CHRIS KERR

Citidyll

Broken Sleep Books
brokensleepbooks.com

'Chris Kerr's poems are unsententious structures, crackers of safewords, ejectors of the seats of power. And they're bad to the bone with form: it's been a long time since you so rock and rolled.'

- Adam Crothers

This edition published 2018,
Broken Sleep Books: Cornwall

First published, 2018
Broken Sleep Books: Cornwall
brokensleepbooks.com

Second Edition

Lay out your unrest.

Publisher/Editor: Aaron Kent
Editor: Charlie Baylis

Typeset in UK by Aaron Kent

Broken Sleep Books is committed to
a sustainable future for our planet,
and therefore uses print on
demand publication.

brokensleepbooks@gmail.com

ISBN-13: 978-1721699094

ISBN-10: 1721699090

CONTENTS

CITIDYLL

Citidyll

Herd sheep down Broadway.
Holy cow, how whimsical!
Something out of a musical.
But New York's been natural for years:
scarred by lanced implants
and tired of being female.

Manhattan ants are zeroes
cinched to infinity by suicide belts.
An individual at Citibank with a sickle.
Totally apolitical. To celebrate
Isis cracks a tray of ice spheres.
A roll of the ice and your head
disappears.

The dead catch icicles in Arthur Kill.
A doctor filters bodies of water.
High fives get higher to stay dry
over hydroponic weed slaughter.
The Hudson banks go under once
it's all flies and flyover.

Twin Study

Statins from a Manhattan physician
are kryptonite to socialites
reared in their dance teacher's mirror.
Darlings don't sicken,
dose daddy with grapefruit
and hope the contraindication kicks in.

At Staten Island's Fresh Kills Landfill
pigeons bracket gull-wing doors.
September's exceptional rubble
is twinned with Kabul or Mosul—where

Arabic isn't freckled crow's feet.
Still, Wall Street's fill or kill
and the bum who squawks FOK FOK FOK
is terminated hermit.

The inside of Paris Is Burning out

A woman needs a transitional outfit to go
below 14th and back: a casual fur
lined with a trench.
They can't steal a rich inner life.
The runway reveal?
Concorde accordioning
the Costa Concordia cos
we're gonna be in the Hudson.
A man's realness takes off
the Queens housewife behind four locks.
Her daughter's stuffed toy socks inside out
and the walrus is a bear with tusks
so soft they're tumours.
Her brother discovers his leopard
bound in an elephant's trunk.
It didn't change its spots
to cut across Flushing
Meadows. The kid grows
up real twisted.
He needs your fly coat
to fit the zip code.
Flips his knife.

Thames Barrier

A shower hits the city.
Country *douche* moonlights as lube.

Soho's rowboat bounces punters out
gently down the stream
from trafficking

at London Wall.
Dawn cracks all the leaks
beneath the dirty clouds in overalls.

Hygienic swimmers lap
to catch a statue's behind
in the gelid Serpentine.

Breakfast's gentrified
jellied eels.
They electrify them straight
the better to vibrate
the guillotines of Aldgate's eateries.

Pick Up Artists

Body paint's stationery,
statues stationary
and Choo-Choo putties out
of the tube at the station.
Step down from the platform, madam!
PUAs fail to get off at Pimlico.
The women at the museum
laugh in pumice PUMAs
because the floor is lava.

Vauxhall gave Russian
its word for station:
a false generalisation
by the visiting delegation.
But Faulke's Hall
was a great country waiting
room for the city to sprawl in.
London made it late,
old stock hauling freight,
while the Tate Britain pulls ass
from 1500 to the present day.
Find an artist to masturbate
to later. Socks and all.

The Lorelei

Dark matter before us today
is becoming the case.
Let's try experience by memory:
the rare trapezoidal present
left at the limit of Soho's zone
when the Lorelei closed.
(Nostalgia's the strobe
the epileptic fell back on.)
Ground floor Italian
with bags of flour by the door
explained the psychogeographer.

Is that Muriel's breast?
A quadrant of her left bicep in the mural?
Its flaky heft would weigh, but less.

Faye and Giacinto cook and clean
tulpas in a Venn of dreams.

Transference

The mermaid's hair's fibre-optic
beams down distant macaroni.
Her ringlets reflect your phone sex
phonetically
in inner cheesy glaze
while she does her nails.

Cam girl from the waist up
doesn't mean she wades.

Tell her the old tale
your pillow won't understand
in the back of a private ambulance
half in a river
the doors spread
siren still going.

Inland Sea Bride

What if your anima isn't an anime character,
Westerner, high pitched voice vowel shifted
to tickle your shitty 19th century bowel,
but unfemale entrails bad for augury
magic-lanterning a tricky kanji?

Write ningyo, or mermaid, in squid ink,
without drawing cephalopods at any fractal level.
Have a stroke while swimming.
White air-conditioned roar
sucks kelpies hoarse.

Memory autoblots:
tai chi poses
transform like Autobots without breaking bones
till forehead smiles to steering wheel
and women drive in Saudi Arabia.

Hairy Ball Theorem

I spit hairs. The bald analyst recommends Houellebecq from Becquerel's beard. 'It sounds like there's a disrupted flow in your relationship', he says.

You can't comb a hairy ball flat without creating a cowlick.

An invisible vector field of Mars symbols on the sphere of Freud's cranium. The pricks of the arrows tingle with alignment. The cowlick is a single Venus symbol at the top of his head.

Mars lost its magnetic field billions of years ago.

'It is difficult to go against the grain, to tell people what they don't want to hear. Have you read Houellebecq?'

Cows graze along the Earth's magnetic field.

The Venus symbol: crosshairs and eye, not lined up.

These celeb hairstyles will help you overcome your cowlick shame:

Woman as misdiagnosed retinal detachment of the male gaze.

Jordan Peterson is teaching young men how to shave.

Multiplexiglass

i

The gaffer will rip his tape
of multiple dimensions
from the hairs of his combover
and secrete the fourth
which is overtime
round his Stetson.
His is the adhesion
between electricity & magnetism
that inducts the lead
into her arboreal aura.

His union frets over false studio fires.
In bars with Fender chords
the gaffer quells them:

Ich am of woodland
Ant of the HOLLYWOODLAND
Of our land …

His fans are a substation
of his attraction to wire.

The director's chair sags with her absence
sneers the guru from a still-lit corner.
No other vibration
escapes the applause's crack.

Don't stub the gaffer's thunder
i lashes back.

Words curve to the terrain.
The letters of the sign
your gaffer just rigged
ripple from downtown
as they never have
from the lathered vantage
of the chopper's math.
Besides, don't most gaffers in this metropolice
answer to Chief
Lighting Technician?
There's a cover of his number:
the actor practises
meditation right and lives.
She leaves off language
for the bungeed field of breath
the lungs plunge into.

Horseshit, bats *i.*
People get real dissociative on that rebound.
i bet she had a psychotic
break at your camp.
That package of both/ands
leads you by the hand
but let go and you're all demon
a goof ball that tried
to interfere with the gills of a koi.

You're still rattling
but that's your action:
my techniques make nothing happen

on a battlefield.
They let this bar

DISSOLVE

ii

After a party in the hills five of us went back to the guru's
property, which is one room surrounded by three
concentric corridors. In the first corridor nothing
happened and the guru turned to the composer and said
'wait here while we go through that door to chant'. In the
second corridor nothing happened and the guru turned to
the director of photography and said 'wait here while we
go through that door and view the dailies'. In the third
corridor nothing happened and the guru turned to the
director and said 'wait here while we go through that
door and I fuck i'. Nothing happened in the guru's room.

Frame

My stunt double has alibis spooled like the takes I'm not
in: she, who I 'sleep with' with (the fishes, men), was
applying herself to my hair extensions in my trailer on the
night you well rehearse. Those hands reverse the buffets
of an all-day buffet. Her hair is gris with the prosthesis
of my shadow. You should see the choreography as she
possesses my wardrobe. And how tightly, each cut to my
throat. Now, if you please, my beau is waiting, like our
red room—the clot I collapse into after a one shot.
Perhaps the two of you can chat sometime, somewhere
more domestic.

Type

The model posed glassless
in the doorway and said
'make my spine hiss at both ends
like a python in a frying pan.'
The photographer buttoned her nose
till it bled arrows.
She felt lighter, a pintsize down,
though her blood loss veneered her volume.
The photographer exposed smears
drawn from anorexic Type A digits,
meaning you can't use this:
it's personal. It isn't.
It was a male model. Sober too.
He'd always finish his girlfriends' sentences
with words like 'faecal transplant.'

Intrusive Thoughts

Decapitating thoughts
into a net dragged out across the lane
ripping silk that thrashes into May.

His lover is a wife who longs to splay
new fingers under sheets so she can train
decapitating thoughts.

They're running low on pillow talk they say
though riding pillion keeps her halfway sane
in ripping silk that thrashes into May.

One impulse in the garden: flay
fresh petals from her patterned dress's stain.
Decapitating thoughts.

Like in a hallucinogenic ray
pa sees new possibilities in *l'aîn-*
ée. Decapitating thoughts
in tripping silk he thrashes into 'may ...

A Abductee

Levi Bellfield suburbia:
the leafy wheel-lined streets where that murderer hit
out women's wills with a ball-peen hammer.
My girlfriend was ten
when two men offered her a lift.
Those true conurban legends left her
obsessed, trailing psychopaths.

I fell for her on a wrought bench.
The Coronas round our constellations smashed
as her lisp eclipsed mine: 'I'm an alien,
thrown to this rock to know you like
a porn star shooting across a studio's videos.
That's why I snooze, comb gnocchi
and bladder liquor on the first floor.
I make sure the knickers kicked in
bushes came there, like, consensually.'

Psychopathism

She is maybe 22,
like a snake in the zoo
'Gatwick', Craig Raine

She's definitely 21: a snake in a zoot
suit escaped from the eagle's mouth.
Zut alors! Mexican youths
are gorging on pork pie hats.

Men in sailor suits strip
gorgeous fabric from
'sexual psychopaths'
and beat a riot in red.

The aliens love to loiter:
they time travelled from Mexican
California to California.
Their kennings are from Mars,
synonyms from Venus
or Aphrodite. Those two are ours.
Aliens vs. Predators.

Toilet Water Cycle

N°1

Ex-perfume exits the apprentice as piss.
The bell above the door rings porcelain
as a flacon breaks up small enough
to be lapped safely by a dog
unnoticed because clean.
Ruby's owner'll recall
his new ex's natural scent as neutral:
sweat on the gear stick while coasting.
The sharps of a handful of petals
mark the vertices of an odourless gem.

N°2

'Calibrate your receptors,
first to dust, then crushed jasmine.
Proceed to rock salt. Last, seal them to all
but the fermenting bacteria.'
So Jacques Polge learned to smell Grasse.
The perfumer shrinks a boulder on the expanse
to a beach pebble with a splash.

N°3

At 37°C his Coco
has met kiss temperature in the vial.
Such a hot day leaks from the phloem
of full-bodied window flowers

they don't bother with pollen.
Esters evaporate and drip down again
in the bottle, circling a woman's name.
His formula soaks under a thumbnail
on a hard drive, whose fan twirls.

N°4

A pipette of MSG, chased with dry ice,
unsticks smell from taste a touch.
She rips perfumes from the press
of patent library leaves.
The unknown ingredient is the erogenous
pixel she skirts: the doppelgänger
that embitters exes.
Tonight she leaves a flute on her patio.
Two drops freeze like nostrils to the glass.

Acknowledgements

I gratefully acknowledge the editors of the following magazines, where earlier drafts of some of these poems appeared: *Adjacent Pineapple, Blackbox Manifold, HVTN* and *The Literateur*.

'A Abductee' was first published in *It All Radiates Outwards: The Verve Anthology of City Poems*.

'Multiplexiglass' adapts the anonymous poem 'The Irish Dancer'.

Many thanks to Claire Askew, Paul Batchelor, Charlie Baylis, David Caddy, Adam Crothers and Aaron Kent.

LAY OUT YOUR UNREST